American Symbols

Ellis Island

by Terri DeGezelle

Consultant:
Melodie Andrews, Ph.D.
Associate Professor of Early American History
Minnesota State University, Mankato

Capstone
press

Mankato, Minnesota

First Facts is published by Capstone Press,
151 Good Counsel Drive, P.O. Box 669, Mankato, Minnesota 56002.
www.capstonepress.com

Library of Congress Cataloging-in-Publication Data
DeGezelle, Terri, 1955–
    Ellis Island / by Terri DeGezelle.
    p. cm.—(American symbols)
    Summary: A simple introduction to Ellis Island, including its history as the first federal immigration station, as part of the Statue of Liberty National Monument, as a museum, and its importance as a symbol of the United States.
    Includes bibliographical references (p. 24) and index.
    ISBN-13: 978-0-7368-2292-3 (hardcover)   ISBN-10: 0-7368-2292-5 (hardcover)
    ISBN-13: 978-0-7368-4706-3 (softcover pbk.)   ISBN-10: 0-7368-4706-5 (softcover pbk.)
    1. Ellis Island Immigration Station (N.Y. and N.J.)—Juvenile literature. [1. Ellis Island Immigration Station (N.Y. and N.J.)] I. Title. II. Series.
JV6484 .D4 2004
304.8′73—dc21   2002156487

Editorial Credits

Roberta Schmidt, editor; Linda Clavel, designer; Kelly Garvin, photo researcher;
    Eric Kudalis and Karen Risch, product planning editors

Photo Credits

Corbis/Kevin Fleming, cover; Bill Ross, 19
Getty Images/Hulton Archive, 11, 12, 13, 15
Index Stock Imagery/Rudi Von Briel, 5, 21
Library of Congress, 7, 17, 20
North Wind Picture Archives, 9

3 4 5 6 7 10 09 08 07 06

Table of Contents

Ellis Island Fast Facts 4

Symbol of Freedom and Hope. 6

Ellis Island and Fort Gibson. 8

The Immigration Station. 10

Immigrant Inspections 12

The Immigration Station Closes. 14

A National Monument 16

Ellis Island Today 18

Timeline 20

Hands On: Make a Family Tree 22

Words to Know 23

Read More 24

Internet Sites 24

Index 24

Ellis Island Fast Facts

★ Before the late 1770s, Ellis Island had many different names. It had been called Gull Island, Oyster Island, Dyre Island, Bucking Island, and Anderson's Island.

★ Ellis Island was chosen for the site of the first Federal Immigration Station in 1890.

★ A 15-year-old girl from Ireland was the first immigrant to pass through Ellis Island.

★ April 17, 1907, was the busiest day for Ellis Island. That day, 11,747 immigrants passed through the station.

★ Between 1892 and 1954, more than 12 million immigrants went through Ellis Island.

★ The American Immigrant Wall of Honor at Ellis Island honors immigrants who came to America. People can have their ancestors' names written on the wall.

Symbol of Freedom and Hope

Ellis Island is a symbol of freedom and hope. Millions of immigrants came to the United States through Ellis Island. They hoped to start a new life in the United States. Immigrants knew they would have freedom when they passed through Ellis Island.

immigrant
a person who leaves one country to live in another country

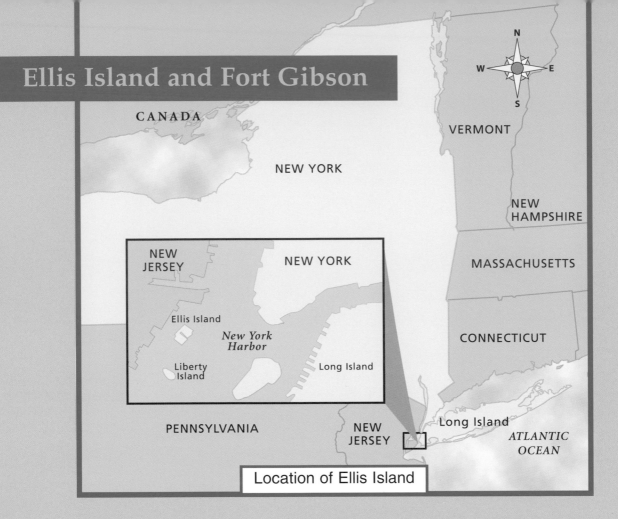

Ellis Island and Fort Gibson

CANADA

VERMONT

NEW YORK

NEW HAMPSHIRE

MASSACHUSETTS

NEW JERSEY

NEW YORK

Ellis Island

New York Harbor

Liberty Island

Long Island

CONNECTICUT

PENNSYLVANIA

NEW JERSEY

Long Island

ATLANTIC OCEAN

Location of Ellis Island

Ellis Island is located in New York Harbor. The island is named after Samuel Ellis. His family owned the island from 1770 to 1808.

In 1808, the United States bought the island. The U.S. government built Fort Gibson there in 1813. The fort was removed in 1861.

The Immigration Station

In 1890, Ellis Island was chosen for the first Federal Immigration Station. The U.S. government built large buildings on the island. Immigrants waited in these buildings before they entered the rest of the country. Millions of immigrants went through the station.

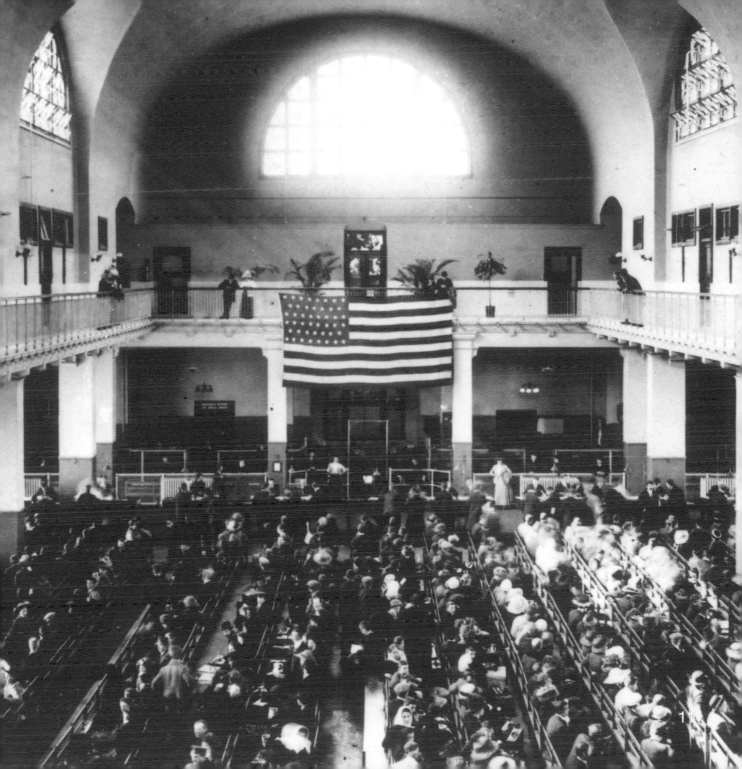

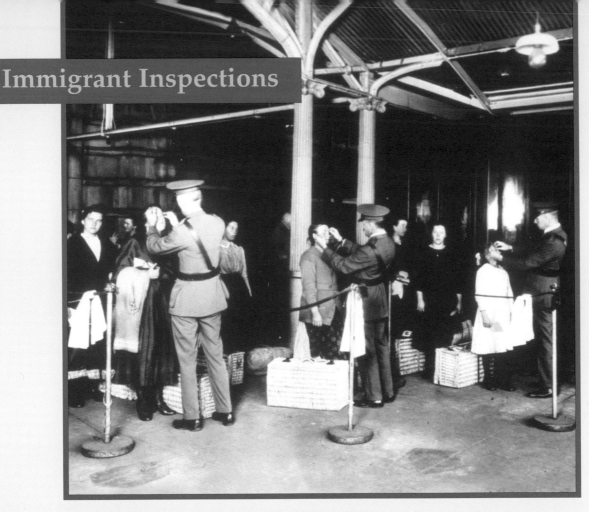

Immigrants had to pass an inspection to stay in the United States. Doctors checked each person. Sick people were sent back to their home country.

Immigrants also were asked about their names and families. Many immigrants did not understand English. This part of the inspection was hard for them.

The Immigration Station Closes

In the 1920s, new laws let fewer immigrants come to the United States. The large station at Ellis Island was not needed. In 1954, the U.S. government closed Ellis Island. Immigrants went to a different station. Ellis Island's buildings became run down.

EXIT

15

A National Monument

In 1965, Ellis Island became part of the nearby Statue of Liberty National Monument. Ellis Island's buildings were repaired. The station became a museum to remember immigrants. The Ellis Island Immigration Museum opened September 10, 1990.

museum
a place where visitors can see historical objects and art

Ellis Island Today

Today, millions of people visit Ellis Island. Many people study their family history there. They can see a list of the immigrants who went through the station. People remember that Ellis Island was a symbol of freedom and hope for their ancestors.

Timeline

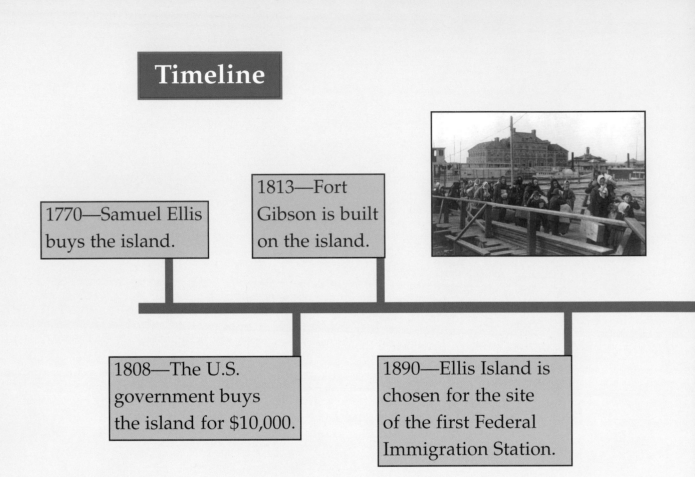

1770—Samuel Ellis buys the island.

1813—Fort Gibson is built on the island.

1808—The U.S. government buys the island for $10,000.

1890—Ellis Island is chosen for the site of the first Federal Immigration Station.

1907—April 17 is the station's busiest day.

1965—Ellis Island becomes part of the Statue of Liberty National Monument.

1990—The Ellis Island Immigration Museum opens.

1954—Ellis Island officially closes.

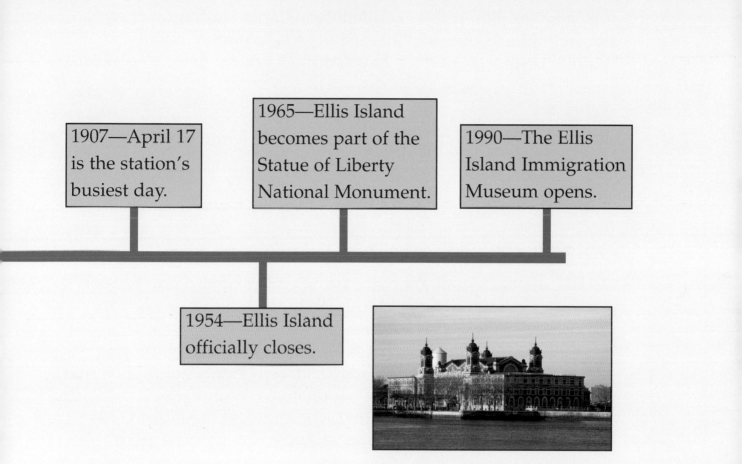

Hands On: Make a Family Tree

Over 100 million people had family members immigrate through Ellis Island. Try this activity to learn more about your ancestors.

What You Need

Markers
Construction paper
Scissors
Glue

Large piece of white paper
Family members
Star stickers

What You Do

1. Use a marker to draw a tree trunk on the construction paper.
2. Cut out the tree trunk and glue it to the white piece of paper.
3. Draw branches on the white piece of paper.
4. Talk to family members. Ask them "When were you born?" "Where were you born?" and "Did you go through Ellis Island?" If none of your living relatives went through Ellis Island, ask them if they knew ancestors who did.
5. Write each person's name on a branch.
6. Put the person's birthday next to his or her name.
7. Print each person's birthplace.
8. Place a star by the names of the people who passed through Ellis Island.

Words to Know

ancestor (AN-sess-tur)—a member of a person's family who lived long ago

freedom (FREE-duhm)—the right to live the way you want

immigrant (IM-uh-gruhnt)—a person who leaves one country to live in another country

inspection (in-SPEK-shuhn)—a test in which something is looked over very carefully

museum (myoo-ZEE-uhm)—a place where visitors can see historical objects and art

symbol (SIM-buhl)—an object that stands for something else

Read More

Klingel, Cynthia Fitterer, and Robert B. Noyed. *Ellis Island.* Wonder Books. Chanhassen, Minn.: Child's World, 2001.

Raatma, Lucia. *Ellis Island.* We the People. Minneapolis: Compass Point Books, 2003.

Internet Sites

Do you want to find out more about Ellis Island? Let FactHound, our fact-finding hound dog, do the research for you.

Here's how:
1) Visit *http://www.facthound.com*
2) Type in the **Book ID** number:
    0736822925
3) Click on **FETCH IT**.

FactHound will fetch Internet sites picked by our editors just for you!

Index

Ellis Island Immigration
    Museum, 16
Ellis, Samuel, 8
Federal Immigration Station,
    10, 14, 18
Fort Gibson, 9
family, 13, 18

freedom, 6, 18
hope, 6, 18
immigrants, 6, 10, 12, 13, 14,
    16, 18
inspection, 12, 13
Statue of Liberty National
    Monument, 16